Mind control technique

The Ultimate Guide to Mastering the Art of Mind Control

Robert N Smith

Table of contents

Introduction

Your mind is a wide arena in which all movement occurs, both inside and outside you. Every day, you have between 50,000 and 70,000 thoughts. The mind continues to do many duties for you at all times. Your mind assists you in functioning normally.

Your life is centered on your thinking, yet little is done to harness the hidden potential of your mind. If no one has ever informed you, if you want to put your life together, you must start with your thinking. When the mind learns to govern itself, it can handle anything.

A relaxed mind is capable of handling any tasks with ease. A disordered mind is caught up in internal and external conflict. When one begins to intentionally spend time in mind management, life begins to govern itself.

But what is the secret to mind management? Each individual has a built-in mechanism for calming the mind, but it is seldom taught how to utilize it. Meditation, breathing methods, and introspection are essential for mind management. A whole new dimension of life opens up if we devote a few minutes of meditation and stillness every day.

"Meditation is sustenance for the soul; it feeds the heart of your being."
- Sri Sri Ravi Shankar, Gurudev

The mind has a tendency to jump back and forth between the past and the future. It is either lamenting or extolling the past, or it is making plans for the future. However, we must recognize that the current instant is a field of infinite possibilities.

Can we take action in the past or in the future? No. We can only act in the present moment, yet while our minds are racing back and forth, we lose track of what we are doing. To make the most use of the present moment, our minds must calm down. Meditation may assist in bringing the mind back to the present moment. It allows us to be present in the moment and respond efficiently.

"Twenty minutes of deep digging within myself provides me with comfort from the ideas that are bothering me at the time. With regular meditation, I've learned to bring my attention back to the present when it's wandering between the past and the future, "Karishma Yadav, a seven-year meditator, agrees.

Meditation's Advantages

- Physical stamina
- Improves concentration and clarity Sharpens attention and awareness
- Increases alertness, improves observation abilities, and makes you lighter.
- Positive vibrations are produced.
- Restorative sleep

Chapter 1

WHY DO YOU REQUIRE MIND CONTROL?

What do you wish to change about yourself? Do you desire more or less of something, to acquire a new skill, or to try new things? Or do you want to make a difference in your relationships, physique, career, or finances?

It doesn't have to imply that you despise your current life or job - you just want it to be better in some manner.

Yes, we all want change, which is WHY you need mind control.

'Mind management precedes life management.' The quality of your thinking influences the quality of your life.' Mr. Robin Sharma

- Your brilliant intellect

Your brain is incredible and powerful. Its fundamental goal is to keep you alive, which it does by keeping you safe, which usually entails preserving the status quo - since that's what has worked so far.

This is great for keeping you alive, but it's not always so great when you want to make changes, or move away from the status quo in some manner.

It's vital to understand that, although you may believe you make your own choices and plans, including what you wish to alter, most of your cognitive processes are unconscious, and decisions are made without you being aware of them most of the time.

This must be done. We have influence over the conscious portion of your mind, which, although fantastic, has limits. It quickly loses attention and normally retains approximately 7 bits of information at once.

This is why the non-conscious mind controls the majority of what happens in your body. It's the engine that propels you, freeing up your conscious mind to concentrate on other things.

- Making a decision

This is vital while making changes because your unconscious mind, which is a million times more powerful than your conscious mind, is in charge. And it does so depending on the ideas and behaviors you've developed throughout your lifetime, not all of which are beneficial to you.

Both aspects of your mind are essential not just for survival, but also for making changes and living the life you choose. The true challenge is getting them to collaborate in order for this to happen.

This allows you to utilize your whole mind to work for you rather than against you;

otherwise, it's all too simple to sabotage what you want to do. That's something we've all done!

Why do you continue to consume foods that you know would not help you get the physique you want when you want to reduce weight? Because your mind is screaming at you that you're hungry and want to eat something delicious. And your intuition and experience tell you that cream cakes, particularly a Victoria sponge with butter cream frosting, will fill you up fast while also tasting delicious. And you've had a long day, so you deserve a small pleasure.

That might be annoying and put you off balance, but it also occurs in critical choices and circumstances. You want to quit your job and start your own company, but your subconscious is shouting at you, 'Are you crazy, you'll never make a successful business person, why do you think you can do it, you never follow through.' Or whatever it is for you depending on your previous experience.

Mind management is the process of being aware of the influence your ideas have on you and learning to use your mind to your benefit.

- Your Opinions

It's time to take a step back, because at the heart of all of this is the idea that the way we think and the ideas we have determine what we do.

Our ideas determine how we feel, which influences what we do or take, which influences how we live our lives.

When you phrase it like that, it seems clear, but take a time to consider if you really believe it or are conscious of it in your daily life.

The actions you perform are the result of your thinking.

As a result, if you alter your ideas (that is, the way you think), you may modify your behaviors. This implies you have the ability to create the changes you want in your life, job, or company.

- You are not your ideas.

It's a fantastic idea to embrace, and it goes hand in hand with the idea that your ideas are things.

You are not your ideas, and your thoughts are not you.

Your ideas do not define you. That is, you may adjust your thinking to help you live the way you want to live. That is what we mean when we say "mind management."

We've discussed why mind management is necessary for change, but it's not simply about doing things differently. It's also about appreciating the simple act of being alive. After all, being happier or more passionate in your everyday life is one of the improvements you may seek.

It's not only about stuff; it's also about 'being.'

And mind control is essential.

Chapter 2

Is it necessary to learn mind management? Yes, you must master mind control to a big degree since we have not been taught how to govern our brains.

We don't study it in school; some institutions do teach things like critical thinking, but that's a different story. At best, we may have learned something about the brain's components and functioning.

Most of us do not acquire it through our natural relationships with our parents, most likely because they did not learn it themselves.

But here is your chance to learn about mind control.

So, how much do we know about the mind? We've discussed the conscious and subconscious mind as two main components of the mind. And we know that our brain is essentially an information processing machine, with nerve cells (neurons) linked by synapses.

What we do, the influences in our life, our prior experiences, beliefs, and values that we have stored in our brains all affect and enhance these neural pathways. And repetition strengthens these brain networks or connections.

One of the possible issues with the mind is that it may be changed intentionally (by your ideas) or subconsciously (by our non-conscious). And the non-conscious (or subconscious) is the more powerful of the two.

We propose that you use mind management to bring the conscious and subconscious minds into harmony. So there is no discord or conflict between the two portions of your brain, as well as between your actions and your beliefs.

That is the key to attaining what you want and creating adjustments, as well as why you want and desire mind management.

You can influence your conscious mind - you can control your ideas - thus you must influence your subconscious mind to connect with the subconscious.

We also know that your subconscious mind was programmed and, as a result, can be reprogrammed, but the process is gradual and incremental.

Your vessel's captain

It's analogous to a super tanker (the subconscious) being piloted by the captain (the conscious).

The captain (conscious mind) may be in command, but the captain's directives take a long time to reach and influence the giant tanker that is our subconscious.

However, repetition may impact the subconscious, just as it can influence the establishment of any habit, including thinking habits.

Advertising focuses on the repetition of essential themes to persuade you to believe in, and then purchase, their product, concept, or ideas.

Because of the power of repetition, you may remember advertisements from years ago, even from your infancy. Especially when you add a few tricks of the trade to make it even more memorable, tactics that we may utilize to our benefit in terms of mind control.

The bottom line is that mind management will assist you in changing what you want to alter and doing what you want to accomplish.

Chapter 3

HOW TO CONTROL YOUR MIND

You control your mind by teaching it to think in certain ways, resulting in the development of habits and ways of thinking that encourage change, happiness, and success for you.

Training your mind may seem far-fetched or like some type of trickery, but it simply refers to the use of strategies and ways of thinking that you may learn through practice.

As a consequence, you may change and modify your life and company by your ideas, beliefs, and actions.

What approaches can assist you in managing your mind?
Among the most important mind management strategies are:

- Setting goals or creating a vision

- Affirmations\Visualization
- Hypnosis
- Meditation and mindfulness
- Repetition and practice are effective methods for learning and internalizing new abilities.

These are the methods we discuss at Brilliant Living HQ and on the Changeability Podcast. In the Changeability framework, they are also recorded in a 10-step structure that demonstrates how they all fit together and build one on the other.

The entire version of this is laid out in a logical practical step-by-step structure on Amazon in the book Changeability: Manage your Mind - Change your Life, which is available in both paperback and Kindle formats. This is the best site to receive a complete explanation and step-by-step instructions.

Mind Management Is Critical

Strong times pass, but tough individuals endure." In today's competitive world, survival has become a difficult undertaking, and many are scrambling to discover a road to success. Be it a student, an employee, a self-employed person, a corporate executive, a politician, or anybody in any walk of life, the success rate in achieving the intended objective is minimal. What drives people to this condition of affairs? The underlying reason is that everyone, as individuals, has a relationship with the outside world. As a result, they are merely relative and not absolute.

This is because most individuals do not look to themselves first before looking to the outside world. They are unaware of their own strengths and potential. They are unable to co-relate because of their flaws. They constantly turn to someone to direct their lives. In the process, they lose their individuality and self-esteem, and their personalities are distorted. They accept loss and never strive to overcome it because they associate their existence with their destiny.

Even successful individuals are often unable to deal with the strains of time, situation, and environment. They are continually stressed and worried as a result of many scenarios. It has an impact on both their body and psyche. It causes depression, which has a negative influence on their lives and performance. The unfavorable consequences are solely the result of their mental attitudes toward their life and surroundings. People forget that "success or failure is determined more by my mental attitudes than by my cerebral ability." "No situation or group of circumstances is a tragedy to be dreaded in and of itself." It is our attitude to it that determines whether it is a "waterloo" or a "field of victory."

The power of the mind over the body has already been scientifically proven. People, however, do not understand how to utilize their mental capacity to their advantage in order to thrive in life. If individuals can grasp and discover their own inner power and potential for what they are capable of accomplishing, then achievement becomes a routine, a habit, and a way of life.

Total Excellence Mind management, particularly in these days of competition and quality, is extremely important and unavoidable, and if performed properly, honestly, and genuinely, may not only bring certain success in life, but also restore order out of chaos in one's life. "In this day and age, it is the power of the mind that dominates the world, and it is obvious that he who has mastered the use of the power of the mind will accomplish the greatest success and reach the highest places that attainment and achievement have in store." The guy who triumphs is the one who can use every aspect of his mental aptitude in real life, and who can make every movement of his mind tell. ”

A healthy, affluent, and smart existence will result from a sound mind in a sound body. A healthy, powerful body and an active, vibrant mind complement each other. However, since the mind is more subtle, its control over the body is more effective and significant. Setting a flawed mind straight is a continual process, and the more consistently it is done, the faster and better the outcome obtained. However, man is complacent and feels that everything is OK with him and that he does not need any improvement since he considers himself to be flawless. His egoistic overconfidence insulates him, blurs his comprehension, and stifles his development. As a result, it is essential to maintain the mental and physical abilities on a constant basis. Body growth is clear and observable from infancy. However, once mature, it stops developing and begins to deteriorate as age catches up with life.

Even though mental development maintains pace with physical development, it does not have to be uniform. It may also be erratic. However, the quality of one's thinking never deteriorates. On the contrary, it matures, becomes more sober, more realistic and practical, more mellows and dependable, and more enlightened and less fallible as a result of life experiences. The mind has the ability to enrich itself till death.

"The natural sciences, physics and chemistry, anatomy and physiology, psychology, and sociology all investigate man as an object." They demonstrate that man is only one link in a long chain of living organisms. He possesses a body and a mind that are his, yet his self is not derived from either of them, despite being the basis of them all. All empirical causalities and biological developmental processes relate to his outward existence but not to himself.

The physical, biological, psychological, and logical components are all facets of his nature, or Kosas, as the Taittiriya Upanishad refers to them. There are many empirical possibilities, but man is more than what he knows about himself." And that is exactly what mind management is all about: seeking the ultimate realization of who he really is.

Chapter 4

Mind management tactics to help you change your life

Are you a rudderless boat thrown about in life's sea, or are you on track to obtain what you want?

Making friends with your mind so it works with you rather than against you is the most effective way to accomplish your objectives and alter your life.

Here are five ideas to get you started. Five ways for controlling your thoughts and getting what you desire in life.

- Mind management Technique 1 - Vision and goal setting "Do you know where you're going, do you like what life is presenting you, do you know where you're going, do you know?" Diana Ross's

The first approach for managing your thoughts to reach your goals in life and business is to know where you're going and what you want to accomplish.

If you don't have any direction or objectives, it's like being in a rudderless boat.

If that's how you want to spend your life, that's OK; we're not suggesting everyone needs objectives; but if you want to change anything about your life, setting goals is a terrific place to start.

These might be long-term or short-term objectives, but the point is to be clear about what you want your life to look like and to have a clear vision so that you can establish your clear intentions.

It's about imagining what your life will be like once you've made those adjustments.

What emotions do you wish to experience? What themes do you wish to live your life by? What terms best describe how you want your life to be?

Make a note of them.

And if you're not sure what you want, what your purpose, mission, or goals are, consider what you would do if money were no issue. What would you do if you had all the money in the world that you could ever need? How would you spend your time?

Another method to approach this is to recall your favorite childhood activities. Before life began to close in on you and you were engrossed in the day-to-day reality of making a job and caring for a home, family, or whatever you believe is impeding you from reaching your aspirations and objectives.

When you've decided what you want to alter or better in your life, write it down.

Return to the original aim and ensure that your objectives are consistent with your beliefs. For example, like myself, you may want to be able to care for your family; to guarantee we have a certain degree of financial stability that enables us to do the things we want to do and live the lifestyle we desire.

But it's not just about the money; the aim must also coincide with my principles. So, for me, it's not only about having money, but also about how that money is gained. Integrity is one of the ideals I want to live by, thus it's critical that my objectives reflect this.

Similarly, it's about being of worth - thus I want to make money by providing value to others, which includes helping them better their lives in some manner.

If all of this seems worthwhile, you may also have values or themes centered on having fun, pleasure, health, well-being, love, and so on.

Just a clue. Consider if your goal is a 'ends or a means' aim while developing your objectives. Is it about what you want to accomplish in the end, or about how you get there?

If you claim you desire more money, is money the end objective, or just a means to an end? For most individuals, money is a means to an end, or the outcome of an end, rather than the end itself.

- 2nd Mind Management Technique - Inventory

Goals are fantastic, but they are insufficient on their own. This is when mind management begins to make a significant impact. You must assess your current situation and determine what is preventing you from accomplishing your objectives.

There are probably self-beliefs and negative notions hiding around in your mind, working hard to keep you exactly where you are today. Nice and safe and secure, at least in your thoughts, even if you may not realize that's where you want to be!

The goal of this strategy is to identify and investigate these limiting beliefs.

Examine your objectives and pay attention to your own response.

Wherever you have a bad sensation or emotional response, repeat to yourself, "This is my aim, but I can't achieve it because..." or "I'll never do that..." or it's not practical... Each of those ideas is accompanied with a restricting negative thinking.

It's your responsibility to capture them and write them down.

You can deal with them once you recognize them. You might tell yourself, "I'm simply thinking those negative and unhelpful limiting ideas," but such thoughts are just that. They are not universal truths, and you may dismiss them.

- Releasing limiting beliefs is the third Mind Management Technique.

Allow it to go. And, no, that's not a musical cue - but it might be.

The objective behind this strategy is to examine and investigate each of these limiting ideas.

Ask yourself why you believe you are thinking this. Is there any reason for this? If there is, do something about it; if there isn't, let it go.

There are several basic approaches that may help you eliminate or reduce the influence of these restricting attitudes and thoughts. Take your list of limiting ideas and break it up into little bits before throwing it in the trash or burning it.

- Empowering Affirmations - Mind Management Technique 4

You replace those negative restricting ideas with positive empowered ones using the fourth of our mind management procedures.

Those restricting ideas are similar to negative affirmations that you constantly tell yourself. So you want to replace them with positive, powerful affirmations to assist you in acquiring and affirming (or making firm) the behaviors, qualities, and activities essential to attain your objectives and create the desired changes.

To do this, write down positive words about how you want to be and read them aloud or aloud again throughout the day.

Write them as if they are already real, since you are brainwashing your subconscious into acting this way right now. You are convincing your subconscious that this is now your new reality, and it will be more inclined to behave in accordance with your desires in this new reality.

Pre-recorded affirmations may be a wonderful benefit to you and a handy method to use affirmations. Listen as frequently as you want till they become second nature to you.

The key is to repeat them often. It's not surprising when you consider how long it took you to accumulate negative affirmations and now you want to accumulate good affirmations. Repeat as many times as you can for as many days as you can, preferably for at least a month.

- Visualization is the fifth Mind Management Technique.

Visualisation is a mind-management approach that requires repeatedly envisioning the intended result (your objectives, your new life).

According to academic research, it's important to also conceive or see the actions required to get there, including conquering hurdles and problems along the way.

Visualization is also known as mental rehearsal, and it is a very common method of mind management used all over the globe to improve an athlete's physical and mental training.

It is also utilized by successful individuals from many areas of life to prepare for and practice the success they want.

Visualization assists in getting you (and your subconscious) in the correct frame of mind to perform what is required to attain your goal.

It does this by seeing or rehearsing in your imagination or mind's eye what you want to achieve and how to attain it in the most realistic manner possible. That includes employing your emotions and sensations, as well as all of your senses as you visualize, including sight, hearing, touch, smell, and taste.

Consider all of this in the current now, as if it were occurring right now rather than some distant future period. This is yet another mind-management technique since the non-conscious does not distinguish between what is actual and what is thought to be real.

A guided visualization may also be used as a fast start visualization to help you get started.

Chapter 5

Tips for Taking Control of Your Mindset and Thought

So you want to master your thoughts. Perhaps you wish to move on from a recent split or are frustrated after a year of physical distance and want to adopt a more positive outlook.

Unwanted ideas may be both frustrating and distressing. You are not alone in wishing them to go. When faced with stress or other problems, it's natural to have difficulty encouraging yourself to look up.

While true mind control is reserved for science fiction, you may attempt to modify your mentality. It may take some work to learn how to restore control, but the ten tactics listed below may assist.

Determine which ideas you wish to modify.

It goes without saying that you must first determine what is on your mind in order to begin to regulate it.

Almost everyone has depressing thoughts or emotional setbacks from time to time. If you're going through a difficult time in your life, you could find it even more difficult to keep control of your spinning thoughts or your entire mood.

Occasional intrusive thoughts are also natural. They may be upsetting, but they usually vanish as swiftly as they came, particularly if you don't interact with them.

Other troublesome thinking patterns might be:

- Rumination, often known as looping thoughts negative self-talk cognitive biases or thinking flaws that might influence your decisions or interactions

- A steadfast gloomy perspective Identifying certain ideas and patterns might help you make the most of the following suggestions.

- Accept unwelcome thoughts Because it's human nature to avoid discomfort, you'd like to avoid ideas that create misery.

- Ignoring uncomfortable ideas is not the way to regain control.
  That typically simply intensifies them.
  Instead, do the opposite: accept and allow those ideas to enter.

- Say you're feeling down because nothing in your life appears to be going as planned, despite your efforts.

Acceptance may include reminding oneself, "Nothing appears to be going right, which is depressing." There's only so much you can do to effect change on your own, but giving up completely isn't an option either."

Acceptance may even reveal why some ideas keep recurring.

Maybe you're still thinking about a fling who abandoned you. Accepting those persistent ideas enables you to realize how much you wanted your relationship to endure.

Their disappearance left you with unanswered questions and an overpowering feeling of inadequacy. You are concerned that you have failed at dating and are hesitant to attempt again.

Recognizing your concerns helps you to face them and remind yourself that you are not to be responsible for their poor behavior.

Keeping the issue in perspective will help you handle your fears of it occurring again rather than allowing worry to prevent you from meeting someone new.

- Attempt meditation.

One excellent method for developing the habit of tolerating undesirable thoughts? Meditation.

Meditation may not seem to assist you manage your thoughts at first, particularly if you are just starting out.You sit and rest, but no matter how hard you try, random ideas keep creeping back up to distract you from the peace you're attempting to attain.

Here are some facts regarding meditation: It can help transform your brain, but you must commit to it.

The challenge is to learn how to sit with the unwanted ideas. You notice them, but you let them go, which helps to weaken their grip on you.

And with that, you've regained some control. The more you meditate, the simpler it is to let go of unpleasant ideas.

Mindfulness meditation, in particular, may help you improve your ability to concentrate on events as they occur.

As you become more conscious, you'll find that you don't have to continually draw your attention away from problematic or distracting ideas.

Meditation has numerous advantages other than better conscious control: it may reduce the intensity of negative emotions and stress, increase resilience and compassion, and even prevent age-related cognitive decline.

- Alter your perception

Self-talk may help you shift your perspective, but the manner you speak to yourself is important.

If addressing oneself in the first person isn't having much of an effect, try moving to a third-person viewpoint. As an example:

Instead of: "I'm unhappy, but I've gone through worse, so I can cope with this as well."
"I realize you're unhappy right now, but you've fought hard to overcome past problems." I believe you have the strength to meet this new challenge as well."
Although it may seem odd at first, this cognitive reappraisal method provides two significant advantages to Trusted Source.

To begin, placing yourself as an outside observer allows you to clear your mind of powerful ideas and emotions. You're removing yourself from a mentality that is simply exacerbating your misery.

When seeing a situation through this freshly distant lens, it is frequently easier to perceive the whole picture rather than simply the most immediate repercussions.

Second, intentionally deciding to study things in the third person allows you to stop circular ideas and effectively investigate your emotions. dependable source

Replace inquiries like "Why do I feel this way?" and "What caused this to effect me so deeply?" when you return your attention to the precise event influencing you. using querics in the third person: "Why does [your name] feel this way?" or "What about this event elicited those emotions?"

Changing your viewpoint tricks your mind into thinking of you as someone else, providing you space from your own difficulties.

This is also useful for encouraging oneself, since individuals prefer to take outward assistance more easily than internal encouragement.

- Concentrate on the good.

Another reappraisal approach that might help you recover control of your thoughts is positive reframing.

Positive thinking does not imply pretending that everything is OK, disregarding issues, or neglecting to examine viable solutions.

Rather, it entails putting a more optimistic spin on your negative ideas – seeking for the silver lining in the storm clouds above.

Reframing will not affect the result of a situation, but it will change how you feel about it.

Assume you slipped in damp leaves while practicing for a race and fell off your bike. You did not receive any serious injuries, although you did break your ankle.

This takes you out of commission for many weeks, leaving you frustrated and annoyed with yourself for riding irresponsibly.

Blaming yourself will almost certainly make you feel much worse. Self-compassion, on the other hand, might help you accept the disappointment and move on to the next chance.

Perhaps you commend yourself for always wearing your helmet, promise yourself that you'll be more prepared for the race next year, or express gratitude that you didn't break anything else.

- Attempt guided imagery.

Guided imagery is a meditation method in which you envision pleasant, tranquil situations in order to achieve a more relaxed state of mind.

A tiny 2014 research found that guided imagery promotes a more pleasant mood and may help relieve stress and anxiety.

You may find it simpler to maintain a relaxed mood and recover control of your thoughts and general mentality once you feel calmer.

- Begin with this easy exercise:

Close your eyes and become comfy – sitting down works best.
Take a few deep, steady breaths. As you develop your visual picture, continue to breathe in this manner.
Create a soothing environment in your imagination by using a variety of sensory elements. Consider what provides you serenity, whether it's the shoreline near your childhood home, a well-worn route in your favorite park, or a lush, crisp fall day.
Include noises, scents, and the sensation of the air on your skin to fully build the scenario.

Imagine yourself going around the scenario you've constructed, taking in every detail and attentively observing your surroundings.
Continue to breathe gently, allowing the tranquility of the sight to wash over you and help you rest.
Enjoy your picture for 10 to 15 minutes.
Finish with a few deep breaths and then open your eyes.
Make a note of it.
Writing down your thoughts may not instantly alter your mood, but it may help you gain control over undesired sentiments.

The act of writing down a notion is frequently sufficient to lessen its intensity. It may be frightening to openly confront and embrace discomfort, but writing things down helps you to address them indirectly.

If you want to go even farther away from painful ideas, consider putting them down in narrative style, as if narrating a tale.

Writing may assist you in becoming more comfortable expressing challenging feelings. Eventually, those undesired ideas may elicit less of a fear reaction, and you may not experience the same level of anguish when they arise.

Try journaling for 15 minutes after a meditation or visualization session. You may write down any ideas that come to mind, happy or bad, while they are still fresh in your head.

Journaling may also assist you in identifying patterns of problematic ideas or actions.

Perhaps you often assign blame after a disagreement with your spouse. This makes you feel horrible about yourself and makes you distrust your interpersonal abilities.

Observing this pattern helps you recognize that you and the other person are equally involved in the disagreement. You vow to be more accountable for your own actions in the future as you move toward more fruitful resolution.

Experiment with targeted diversions.
You won't want to divert yourself on every occasion; it's probably not a good idea to play a game on your phone during a coworker's presentation.

However, in certain cases, targeted diversions might assist refocus thoughts and boost your mood. Certain forms of distractions may actually increase motivation and productivity.

Assume you're feeling depressed and out of sorts since your hiking vacation has been postponed due to a week of terrible weather. You're unhappy because you can't do what you planned, so you focus on things you've been meaning to do.

Completing a library book, tidying your room, and organizing old clothing for donation all make you feel like you've made the most of your time. This motivates you to do more tasks before leaving.

Other possible positive distractions include:

- spending time with family and friends
- listening to uplifting or soothing music
- going for a stroll
- Just make sure you're utilizing diversions as a momentary respite and not as a form of denial or avoidance.

Chapter 6

Work on stress management.

When situations outside your control add stress to your life, it may be challenging to maintain your mental health.

Anxiety and stress may foster unpleasant ideas. This may cause further anxiety, creating a vicious cycle that can quickly become unbearable.

Begin regaining control by investigating important causes of stress in your life and looking for possible strategies to eliminate or lessen those triggers.

Most individuals are unable to entirely eliminate stress causes. Outside causes of stress are common. You don't always have control over what occurs around you.

This is where self-care comes into play. Setting aside time to nourish your mind and body may boost overall well-being. It also makes it simpler to recover from life's adversities with a more optimistic view.

Self-care may include:

- Getting enough sleep, eating nutritious foods, maintaining social connections, and creating time for relaxing

- Learn how to create a tailored self-care strategy.

- Consult a therapist.

It is often easier said than done to learn to manage your thoughts.

The suggestions above may not make a significant impact for long-term mental health disorders and symptoms such as:

Obsessions and compulsions caused by depression
recurring or intensifying intrusive thoughts about others extremely suspicious or unfavorable thoughts about others
prolonged anguish or despair
Seeking expert help for any attitude that is affecting your relationships and general well-being is worthwhile. A therapist may assist you in identifying underlying difficulties and exploring possible solutions.

Therapy also gives you a chance to work on self-compassion and encouraging self-talk, both of which are helpful strategies for taking back control of your attitude.

If a therapist offers the following services, seek them out:

Acceptance and commitment therapy (ACT) is a mindfulness-based cognitive therapy that is a component of cognitive behavioral therapy (CBT).
psychological counseling
These techniques were specifically created to help people improve their ability to accept, challenge, and reframe unhelpful beliefs.

In summary
To have control over your thoughts, you don't need to be psychic. Perhaps all you need is some patience and practice.

A therapist could be of assistance if you struggle to take back control of your thoughts.

Observe These Straightforward Guidelines to Become a Master of Your Thoughts

You will develop into what you envision.

A Bruce Lee

Our thoughts have a big impact on our actions. Thoughts come first and serve as the foundation for all we do and say. Simply put, if you imagine achievement, you will inevitably feel motivated to reach the goals. On the other side, fostering negativity and procrastination will only result in emptiness. How you intend to envision yourself in the near future is significantly influenced by the layer of thinking you are operating in. We are exposed to both positive and negative stimuli in our thinking. You will therefore gather both positive and bad thoughts as a result. The challenge is motivating yourself to think positively while training your mind to weed out negative thoughts.

You will learn some simple recommendations in the following post that will help you master your own thoughts.

1. Develop the skill of pausing.

Our minds are constantly buzzing with thoughts. Not all ideas are valid, and if they are promoted, they could result in undesired conduct. Therefore, stop before encouraging any thought to advance. When you're feeling especially excited or anxious about something, it's especially important. Think about whether it is suitable to direct your attention in that particular direction. Your subconscious knows everything and will always give you the right answer. When we pause, we might collect our thoughts and feelings, which would help us see the situation more clearly. Practice stopping before letting your thoughts run wild as a result. You'll find it helps you stop negative thoughts and think positively.

2. To regain control of your thoughts, practice deep breathing.

Sometimes we can't stop ourselves from acting in inappropriate ways. We simply couldn't stop thinking bad ideas, which is why we did it. You must first learn to control your ideas if you wish to manage them for positive outcomes. A great way to manage your thoughts is by deep breathing. When you become aware that your thoughts are becoming out of control, quickly alert your mind. Remind yourself to stop and relax. Then, while taking 7–11 deep breaths, try not to think about anything in particular. Experts advise practicing deep breathing for at least 90 seconds.

Take several long, deep breaths to give your mind a brief break from racing ideas and give yourself time to collect your thoughts before rethinking. The entire procedure will assist you in preventing undesired thoughts and allowing just "should-thinking" thoughts.

3. Attempt to comprehend the sources of challenging thoughts.

Sometimes it's impossible for us to stop thinking bad thoughts that keep us from using our minds in a productive way. These could be caused by certain triggers that unintentionally or intentionally encourage negative thoughts in you. It can be the sight of someone who has been very harsh toward you. It could also be a location or circumstance that makes you feel fearful, uneasy, insecure, or utterly vengeful. Your job is to identify those triggers and respond appropriately. Once you've found them, consider whether you have any control over them. If so, carry it out. Try to avoid those triggers if you are powerless to stop them.

4. Engage in meditation.

Meditation, a practice of saints and monks, is the earliest method of gaining control over your mind. A disturbed, agitated mind produces disturbed, bad ideas. You must take charge of your mind before you can master your own thoughts. Here's where meditation comes into play. The ancient technique helps you attain mental clarity by calming down your brain. Positive thoughts are encouraged and undesired and negative thoughts are prevented by a stress-free, stress-free mind. A daily session of 5 to 10 minutes would be sufficient. Today, there are many different meditation apps available, and you can even locate online meditation guides.

5. Promote feeling upbeat
When you internally feel good, you think good thoughts and behave good. So make an effort to surround yourself with things that make you feel good. As previously stated,

you get the same result with your ideas when you make yourself feel a certain way. Learn inspirational sayings and tales that can motivate you to think positively and constructively. Find those who make you feel optimistic. To promote such goodness in your life, make an effort to be with them. It will always result in optimistic thinking.

6. Look for motivation for desired ideas
The challenge is to identify what will cause you to focus your thoughts in the direction of the behavior you desire. For instance, you could want to focus your thoughts to motivate you to study hard if you want to get good grades. You must therefore surround yourself with items that will encourage you to think positively.

7. Avoid dwelling on the past.
It serves no purpose to dwell on previous occurrences that were out of your control. The more you give yourself permission to dwell on uncontrollable things, the more

control you lose over your thoughts. You must realize that there are some things for which there is nothing you can do. You must come to terms with this essential truth and have a good outlook moving forward. You cannot direct your thoughts in the desired direction unless you give yourself permission to emerge from the ashes.

8. Trust in yourself and use visualization
Another excellent method for directing your thoughts toward the fulfillment of your dreams is visualization. You must persuade yourself to believe in your aspirations and objectives. Such assurance will motivate you to form desired thoughts, which will then motivate you to behave appropriately. Encourage yourself to picture what you want to become or accomplish. Strong visions will prime your mind to consider the strategies and tactics required to reach those goals.

Additionally, you ought to prioritize looking after your mental wellbeing. Maintain a healthy, balanced diet, stay hydrated, get enough sleep, and discourage wicked thoughts. Don't forget to pause when necessary. A calm, balanced mind is usually simpler to control and master than an anxious, disordered mind.

www.ingramcontent.com/pod-product-compliance
Lightning Source LLC
LaVergne TN
LVHW050343160826
845677LV00014B/3756
* 9 7 9 8 3 5 3 0 3 6 3 3 3 *